How To Have Victory In Life

A practical guide to walking in the supernatural power of God

BARRY YOUNG

D1059299

ISBN: 1975955056
ISBN 13: 9781975955052
Library of Congress Control Number: 2017914914
CreateSpace Independent Publishing Platform
North Charleston, South Carolina

DEDICATION

This book is dedicated to two men who have been instrumental in my life and ministry.

I want to thank Pastor Larry Block and the entire Block family. Pastor Block has been an inspiration, encouragement, and mentor to me in so many ways. Every person he meets encounters the love and power of Jesus through the way he lives his life. Pastor, you are a hero and general in the faith! I deeply love you and your entire family.

I also want to thank Pastor Skip Ethridge. Pastor Skip, you are using every attack the enemy has thrown at you and using it for God. Your boldness, bravery, and compassion inspire me so much. Thank you for your friendship. I deeply love you and Kathy.

ACKNOWLEDGMENT

I deeply love and appreciate these incredible people for their support, wisdom, and godly direction. They have been invaluable to my life!

Kelly Young: Thank you for all of your love, support, and wisdom. Your hard work on this project and all the projects I do is priceless. I am so thankful God has allowed me to be ministry partners with you and, more importantly, life partners. I love you!

Pastor Bill Newby: The time I was able to serve on staff with you is so precious to me. I quote you all the time. There were many times when I would hug you that I felt like I was hugging Jesus. Thank you for the deep impact you have made on my life.

Jason Cooley: You have been a brother to me! I always have your back, and I know you always have mine. When I read Proverbs 18:24, I think of you. Thank you for your years of friendship and brotherhood.

TABLE OF CONTENTS

FACTS ABOUT YOUR LIFE

Science can't answer the three most important questions we have in life: Where did we come from? Why are we here? Where will we go when we die?

Friend, it isn't an accident that this book is in your hand. One day you are going to die, and so will I. Are you walking with God? Are you right with God? Have you asked his Son Jesus Christ into your life? There is absolutely no way you, by yourself, can earn eternal life! The Bible clearly states in Romans 3:23, "All have sinned." The Bible also clearly states in Romans 6:23, "For the wages of sin is death." We will all die, and if we do not receive the gift of eternal life found only in Jesus, we have nothing to look forward to but physical death and then an eternity separated from God. There is, however, hope!

PRAYER OF SALVATION

Having eternal life with God is not about a religion, it is not about a specific church, and it is certainly not about the efforts of humankind. Having eternal life is about a person: Jesus Christ.

If you would like to receive Jesus Christ as Lord, he can save you, forgive you, heal you, love you, and most importantly, give you eternal life. The Bible says in Romans 10:9–10, "If you confess with your mouth the Lord Jesus and believe in your heart that God has raised him from the dead, you will be saved. For with the heart one believes unto righteousness, and with the mouth confession is made unto salvation." If you would like to receive eternal life, would you pray this prayer?

> *Lord Jesus, right now I call on your name. I ask you to be the Lord of my life. I ask you to forgive me for all of my sins. I confess with my mouth and I believe in my heart that you died on the cross and rose from the grave. I receive your love and your salvation.*

Friend, if you prayed that prayer in faith, you are now a Christian. If you are not in a Bible-believing church, start attending one now. As believers, we need one another. If you prayed this prayer, would you contact our ministry at www.servingpastors.com? We would love to hear your story.

INTRODUCTION

This book is not meant to be a theological exposé on topics that aren't relevant for today. This book is not meant to tickle your ear and make you laugh. This book was written to help you have a greater understanding of one amazingly powerful truth: *God wants you to daily have victory in your life!*

Consider what Jesus says in John 10:10: "The thief does not come except to steal, and to kill, and to destroy. I have come that they may have life, and that they may have it more abundantly." Did you catch the end of this verse? Jesus is declaring that he came to give us abundant life. Sadly, many Christians aren't truly living the abundant life that God desires for them to have. Instead, numerous Christians are living the absent life, which is a life that lacks the overflowing blessings of God.

Let's examine what the Old Testament reveals when lives are fully committed to God. Reflect on Proverbs 16:3: "Commit your works to the Lord, and your thoughts will be established." Praise God! I am excited that this verse and so many like it are in the Bible. God wants us to have success. However, abundant life and victory only occur when our lives are lived in the power of God and are focused on the God of the power. When our lives are committed to Jesus, God pours out his blessings on us.

So many precious believers are living in the land of "good enough." For example, when they are asked, "How is your marriage?" they respond with, "It isn't great, but it is good enough." When they are questioned about their finances, they might say, "We are living paycheck to paycheck, but it is good enough." You may even hear someone ask them, "Is your walk with God alive?" to which some may reply, "I wish I had more time to read the Bible and pray, but it is good enough." Friend, God wants us to abandon the life of "good enough" and instead live a life filled with more than enough!

It doesn't take real faith to just get by and accept whatever might be thrown your way in life. However, it does take genuine faith to boldly declare, "I will have victory in my life." I am not saying you won't have bad days or moments when you might feel defeated. However, what I am saying is God wants you to have victory in your life regardless of any trial you may face. The only thing standing between you and a life filled with victory and adventure is *you*!

Joshua 24:15 says, "Choose for yourselves this day whom you will serve." Starting today, would you make the courageous choice to boldly declare that your life is going to be filled with God's victory? Would you take a faith step and proclaim, "I don't care what has happened in the past; but I am going to have everything God wants me to have today"?

Throughout this book, we are going to examine the famous Bible story of David and Goliath, as well as look at some core Bible principles about how to have victory in life. We are going to study the actions and choices of the youngest son of Jesse, David, a young boy who was not even fully grown when he faced the giant, Goliath. He was the only one who stood up to the giant when thousands of warriors from the nation of Israel were too afraid. A teenage boy was used by God to do what an entire army could not do: defeat the giant. Please let the Word of God open your eyes to the fact that you can slay every giant in your life!

You can have victory in life if you live life God's way. Be blessed!

Barry

1

DON'T FOCUS ON THE SIZE OF THE PROBLEM

"And a champion went out from the camp of the Philistines, named Goliath, from Gath, whose height was six cubits and a span."

1 Samuel 17:4

"Let no man's heart fail because of him; your servant will go and fight with this Philistine."

1 Samuel 17:32

"Then all this assembly shall know that the Lord does not save with sword or spear; for the battle is the Lord's, and he will give you into our hands."

1 Samuel 17:47

Does size matter? For the nation of Israel, it sure did. A giant warrior named Goliath wanted to steal, kill, and destroy God's people. You would have thought with all of the miracles God's people had experienced, one of the Israelites would have stepped up in boldness to come against the giant. Or, perhaps the army of Israel could have even considered cheating, where possibly two men would attempt a sneak attack against this Philistine champion. Nope, this thought didn't even cross their minds. There wasn't anyone in God's army who would step up to challenge the giant.

Oftentimes, believers today respond to trials in the same way the Israelite army did. Many of us have experienced God's miracle-working power and have seen God do amazing things. However, sadly, when the giants rise up in our lives, we start depending on someone else to save us instead of trusting God to give us the victory. We as believers might cry out to a family member or a friend, or even call upon our pastor to fight the giant for us. However, the truth is all believers can face the giants that come against them.

As we look further into the story of David and Goliath, we see that in the absence of a strong warrior standing up for Israel, all that could be heard were the shouting threats of the enemy. That is, until the hero of the story stepped in: a young boy who had never served in the army wanted a chance to go after this killing machine, Goliath. David raised his hand to volunteer when nobody else in the entire nation would.

David was the youngest of eight brothers. Can you imagine how many times he might have been picked on by his older siblings? Consider all the dog piles, Dutch rubs, and roughhousing that might have occurred in his family. Wow! I wonder how many times his brothers pinned him down in a wrestling match and made him cry uncle.

When David stepped up and said he wanted to fight Goliath, I can only imagine that his brothers might have been thinking this thought: "If David can't beat us at home, then how in the world can he defeat this giant?" To be honest, that is a really good and fair question. However, the answer can be found in David's heart. His brothers were looking at his natural ability. David was viewing this giant through his muscle of faith, not through the muscles of his own strength! Let's look deeper at the response of David.

David Didn't Call Goliath A Giant

You can examine this story as many times as you want, but you will never read a verse where David calls Goliath a giant. The Bible says Goliath's height was "six cubits and a span." According to today's measurements, Goliath would be about nine feet tall. However, notice that David never describes or views Goliath as a giant. David had a balanced, God-centered perspective about Goliath. Many of us go to the extremes when it comes to our own personal giants. It seems that we either ignore our giants by hiding our heads in the sand, or we tend to magnify and talk up our giants. I have seen some Christians spend more time talking about how big and bad their problems are than on how good and loving their God is. When we spend more time talking about our problems than the goodness of God, I can promise that you will begin to feel defeated by those giants.

While David could see the size of Goliath, he never used his words to magnify Goliath's image. The devil wants you to talk about your problems. The devil wants you to call the trials you are facing right now "giants." It is okay to identify your trials, but don't idolize them. Don't use your own negative words and energy to focus and make a problem intended to harm you even bigger.

David was eager to face Goliath. While the entire nation of Israel saw a giant, David saw an opportunity. David saw an opportunity for God to use him to show his people that he loved them and would protect them if they would only put their trust in him. David magnified God, while the

Israelites magnified the problem. Look at what David says to Saul in 1 Samuel 17:32: "Let no man's heart fail because of him; your servant will go and fight with this Philistine."

I am sure every solider in the Israelite army was surprised to see David willing to fight Goliath. I am also confident every solider in the Philistine army was caught off guard to see that David was willing to fight Goliath. I even think Goliath was shocked to hear that a scrawny shepherd boy wanted to step into the ring with him.

Let me ask you: What trials are you facing today? Can you identify the issues in your life that you are calling a giant? Instead of running from your problems, would you consider running to and facing the giant? In 1 Samuel 17, we can see that David ran toward Goliath without fear. When you run from your troubles, you become powerless. When you run to them with the Lord's help, you are powerful! God wants you to prevail!

David Knew He Needed To Have Saying Power In Order To Have Seeing Power

Let's examine what this brave shepherd boy says in 1 Samuel 17:47: "Then all this assembly shall know that...he will give you into our hands."

It is one thing for David to have the courage to take on the bully. But it was a different thing altogether for

David to confidently announce to all the people that he was not only going to fight this defiant intimidator but also take him down and be victorious. Wow! That is some real boldness!

David began to speak positive, faith-filled words. We get in trouble when we stand on our own words. But David wasn't taking a stand on his own words. David was taking a stand on the faithfulness of God. In 1 Samuel 17:36, when David says, "Your servant has killed both lion and bear," he was recounting the blessings and victories God had given him prior to this encounter with Goliath.

It is incredible how powerful we become when we just start meditating on how God has shown up to help us in times past. When I slow down and start recalling God's faithfulness to me time after time, I become thankful. I am also energized and confident to take greater steps of faith because God has always been with me, and he never lets me down!

David began to speak faith because he was able to bring to memory the goodness of God throughout his life. Would you do likewise? When you are facing financial hardships, would you spend time remembering how God provided for you in the past? If you are facing health problems, would you reflect on the times in the past when God protected and healed you?

You can't have a positive life and a negative mouth. If you want to have victory, you need to be able to speak victory. If you want joy, you need to speak joy. It is easy to grumble and complain. However, I don't want you just to confess positive things; I want you to agree with what the Bible says about you. For example, Philippians 4:13 states, "I can do all things through Christ who strengthens me." The next time you face a trial, simply speak this verse out loud: "I agree with Philippians 4:13 that 'I can do all things through Christ who strengthens me.'" The moment you start declaring God's Word in faith and begin to just agree with what God says about you and your situation, the gates of hell will shake. The devil does not want you to comprehend God's Word or to agree with what God says. Instead, the devil wants you to agree with his lies, such as "Your marriage is over," or "You won't ever get out of debt." Please say yes to God and no to the devil.

Don't focus all your time talking about the problem. Spend your time talking about the answer. Genesis 1:1 says, "In the beginning God created the heavens and the earth." If God created the heavens and the earth, then he can create an answer for whatever giant you may be facing today.

There is so much power in our words. Proverbs 18:21 says, "Death and life are in the power of the tongue."

Look at the way Jesus used his words. Jesus spoke to his Heavenly Father, the devil, and the people he encountered. But have you ever considered that Jesus also spoke to the wind, waves, trees, evil spirits, and sickness? When Jesus spoke, he was declaring the good news. He wasn't speaking about any of the trials he may have been facing; instead, he was always speaking about the goodness of God.

You can have immeasurable victory in your life, but you won't get that victory doing things your own way. When we try to take charge of our finances, marriages, and destinies, we will struggle and be defeated every time. However, thank God the opposite is true. When God is in charge of every area of our lives, we will be blessed and have victory.

Consider the fact that none of the warriors from Israel would stand up to fight Goliath. King Saul, who had previously been used by God to bring Israel great victories, wouldn't stand up to Goliath. Even though Saul had seen and experienced God's power in the past, he refused to trust God when faced with this giant. Why? Because Saul, the Israelite army, and David's brothers were all focused on the size of this Philistine giant, Goliath. David was the only one willing to challenge Goliath because instead of focusing on the size of the giant, he was focused on the size of his God!

We can apply this example to our own lives. You will never get victory in your marriage if you are focused on the size of the argument. You will never get victory in your finances if you are focused on the size of your debt. There is no hope for victory in your physical body as long as you focus on the size of the health problem. Victory will be yours when you focus on the size of your God.

Are you calling your problems giants or opportunities? Are you talking more about your problems than about your God? Are you focused on the problem or the answer? You can have victory in your life, but only if you:

- View your problems as opportunities.
- Speak words that agree with what God has already said.
- Focus on the size of your God, instead of focusing on the size of the giant.

2

DON'T LISTEN TO THE CRITICS

"And Saul said to David, 'You are not able to go against this Philistine to fight him; for you are a youth, and he a man of war from his youth.'"

1 Samuel 17:33

The definition of a *critic* is a person who expresses an unfavorable opinion of something.

The moment you desire to start having daily victory in your life, there is one such critic, the devil, who will try to defeat you by criticizing everything you do. Even after you have gained ground against the enemy and start experiencing daily victory in your life, there can be supposedly "well-intentioned" people who become jealous and start responding critically to you.

Look at what King Saul says in 1 Samuel 17:33: "You are not able to go against this Philistine to fight him." Did you just read that critique against David? You would think Saul would be relieved to discover that someone on Israel's side wanted to attempt to defeat Goliath after all his other soldiers backed down in fear. However, the moment David stepped up and said he was willing to fight the giant, Saul criticized him in hopes of discouraging him from entering the ring against Goliath.

Sadly, today, I have heard of instances where supposedly "well-intentioned" Christians developed websites for the sole purpose of criticizing and attacking successful preachers. Oftentimes, God was using these ministers to share the good news to the masses. The Lord taught me a lesson a long time ago that I needed to save my bullets for the devil. In any of my books, CDs, podcasts, or radio broadcasts, you will never hear me criticize another preacher. If

God wants a pastor to be humbled, he will be the one to do so. Our job is not to judge or critique other Christians; our responsibility is to defeat the devil by praying for one another. Our job is not to divide the church but to encourage it. Can I motivate you to save your bullets for the devil? Don't waste your precious time on Earth attacking another ministry; but instead, preach the gospel of Jesus with love and begin attacking the kingdom of darkness.

When Others Give You Vision, It Is Always Too Small

Saul had the vision to be king but not the revelation to protect his kingdom. David was one of the greatest warriors in the history of the world, but Saul couldn't see it. The man who would make Israel a large and powerful nation was right under Saul's nose, but he didn't even notice. If you are walking with God, you have his supernatural power on the inside of you regardless if other people see it or not. All that matters is that you are aware of God's power in your life and that you act upon it.

Basically, if you allow anyone to speak vision over your life, it will always be too small. Of course, God will use other people to correct us, to hold us accountable, and to bring clarity and confirmation. However when God has a plan, vision, or dream for you, he will always directly share that revelation with you. If you want to know what you are supposed to do in life, in your trial, or in any area of your life, seeking another person will never work. We must go directly to God and trust him to direct our steps.

We all need godly men and women in our lives to help train and sharpen us. However, the greatest leaders teach those in their sphere of influence not to be dependent on themselves but instead to be dependent on God alone. When other people share what they believe to be a vision for your life, remember they can only see the here and now. But when God speaks to you about his vision for your life, he sees all of eternity. If you only listen to another person's vision for your life instead of God's, it could greatly minimize the impact God wants you to have on this world.

There is no quick and easy answer. If you want to know God's vision for your life, you have to seek God. Jeremiah 29:13 says, "You will seek me and find me, when you search for me with all your heart." God demonstrates throughout his Word that he wants to talk to his people, but we have to listen. God wants to speak to you!

When God Gives You Vision, It Is Always Too Big

When God speaks to you, often his vision will be so big it could terrify you. Praise God! God's vision for you is colossal. There are times when people make hearing God's voice strange or weird. However, God's Word is his will. Throughout the Bible, we can see God asking and encouraging his followers to take crazy steps of faith. He asked Daniel to step into the lion's den. He led Shadrach, Meshach, and Abednego into a fiery furnace. He asked Peter to walk on water. There is one sure way to know when God is speaking, because he will likely ask you to do things you can't do in your own power. We serve a miracle-working, all-powerful God.

God has a plan for every single person on this planet. However, he will not empower you to become like Billy Graham or your pastor. When you submit to God, he will empower you to become the victorious *you* he created you to be. Victory is only made possible when we spend the time to personally meet with God and be in his presence. We need to make sure we have heard God speak and then take action. God has an amazing adventure in store for you. Don't let other people give you their secondhand vision for your life. Instead, go directly to God and seek his firsthand vision and plan for your future.

The invisible is invaluable! When you truly begin listening to God, he will share his significant and powerful vision with you. I believe if you aren't a little frightened by what God has shared with you, you may not have truly heard what he revealed to you. This world is hurting, and God needs people who are ready to believe in him for God-sized dreams. I truly believe God wants to show his love and mercy to this entire world. Oftentimes, God uses people to heal hurting people. Ask God how he can use your life to make a difference, and when he speaks to you, make sure to act on what he tells you to do.

Consider that God's plan for David was for him to defeat a nine-foot-tall giant. David could not accomplish this feat in his own power. No one on the battlefield representing either the Israelite or Philistine armies could envision what victory David was about to achieve. But God had an amazing surprise that day for those on the battlefield! David was the only one who knew what that surprise was, and he acted on the vision God gave him to triumph over the enemy!

3

BELIEVE FOR THE IMPOSSIBLE

"This day the Lord will deliver you into my hand, and I will strike you and take your head from you."

1 Samuel 17:46

"Then all this assembly shall know that the Lord does not save with sword or spear; for the battle is the Lord's, and he will give you into our hands."

1 Samuel 17:47

Believing for the impossible is not a simple concept. If it were easy to trust God for miracles, everyone would be a believer. As we look at the story of David and Goliath, we notice a whole cast of characters who were *not* believing for the impossible: David's older brothers, the tough warriors serving in the Israelite army, the arrogant Philistine army and their giant, Goliath, and finally King Saul had trouble believing God for the impossible. Saul's lack of faith is amazing, especially when we consider his successful military track record and all the victories God gave him in the past.

1 Samuel 14:47 states, "So Saul established his sovereignty over Israel, and fought against all his enemies on every side, against Moab, against the people of Ammon, against Edom, against the kings of Zobah, and against the Philistines. Wherever he turned, he harassed them." After rereading the last part of this verse, we come to the realization that God made Saul so powerful he was defeating a multitude of different enemies of God's people. Wherever Saul turned, God gave him victory in every battle he faced.

Despite all of these victories and witnessing God do the impossible in his life, King Saul was still terrified of Goliath. Despite all his past accomplishments, he was paralyzed to face off against Goliath. And sometimes we, as believers, are like Saul in that we forget the countless times when God has prevailed and given us victories in the past.

Right now, if you are facing a giant, would you learn from King Saul's mistake? Would you make a focused effort to recall from your past all of the many ways God showed up and performed miracles on your behalf? Take a moment, lay this book down, and truly reflect on how God has intervened for you in the past. It might even help to write down these memories so you can read back through them anytime you are facing a giant.

Hebrews 13:8 says, "Jesus Christ is the same yesterday, today and forever." If God has done mighty acts in your past, why wouldn't he do the same today? Don't follow in King Saul's footsteps of having a short-term memory of the past victories God has given you. Our past is not a place of residence; it is a point of reference. Use your past to remember and reference the victories, the miracles, and the ways God has stepped in and shown you his love!

You Can't Change Your Life Until You Change Your Thinking

What was David thinking when he challenged Goliath? We know exactly what he was thinking, according to David's own words in 1 Samuel 17:46: "This day the Lord will deliver you into my hand, and I will strike you and take your head from you." In my opinion, David had powerful thoughts behind the words of victory he spoke.

Basically, David had thoughts of victory before he actually accomplished the victory. It can be very difficult to make changes in your life until you make changes to your thinking. Changing your thinking requires courage and is a heroic action that takes faith, guts, and a complete lack of regard for other people's opinions.

Where do you need to change your thinking? I read an old story where the ruler of Russia, Catherine the Great, gave orders for the military to guard a remote section of the property grounds. Her request was for guards to rotate in and out, day and night, twenty-four hours a day. Year after year, for over one hundred years, the military honored the request to guard this area. Finally, someone investigated further as to the reason behind guarding this remote section on the property. It turned out that Catherine the Great was given a special rosebush for her garden, so after it was planted, she gave orders for this bush to be guarded at all times to prevent anyone from disturbing or destroying it.

However, after one hundred years, the rosebush and Catherine the Great had long been dead! During those many years, the Russian military allocated time, money, and resources to protecting something that was no longer there. Generations of leaders and soldiers were guarding something that no one even knew of or understood what they were protecting. To say the military was in a rut concerning this situation is an understatement.

I mention this story because it represents a picture of how our thinking can work today. Many times with our thinking, we try to keep something that is dead alive again. We find ourselves simply wasting time on something that is no longer living. How many of us waste time, God's most precious asset given to us, on something that is way past its life cycle? Where do you need to change your thinking? Where do you need a reality check? What is that activity you are engaged in that you need to walk away from? Sometimes we can have the right energy on the wrong area of focus.

The reality is that if you *think* you are going to lose, you will probably lose. If you *think* you won't get the job, there is a good chance you won't land the job. If you *think* it is impossible for you to start your own business, then you probably won't ever get around to establishing that new business. If you want things to change in your life, your marriage, your finances, or your dreams, you need to have the courage to change your thinking.

An example of how our thoughts can affect reality can be seen with the issue of eating disorders. Sadly, a person who struggles with an eating disorder might weigh under one hundred pounds, but when that person looks in the mirror, he or she views him or herself critically as being overweight. These inaccurate and distorted thoughts become that person's reality regardless of whether it is true or not. As believers, we have to be careful not to accept the lies the devil whispers in our ears as truth for our lives. We have to reject those thoughts and believe God's Word.

How many believers look in the mirror and see a guilty, unclean person, when in reality God sees an innocent, clean son or daughter? How many Christians view themselves as worthless or foolish, when in reality Jesus views each person as having much value and worth, so much so that he gave his life for all? We need to change our thinking and see our lives through God's perspective!

Removing negative thoughts about ourselves is only half the battle. Another major key to victory is to start believing what God says about us. Gaining victory isn't just about thinking positive thoughts about ourselves. Believing we can have victory in life just by thinking positively about ourselves is human-based, powerless, and empty. Instead of thinking positive thoughts, we need to replace negative thoughts about ourselves with the Word of God. We have to replace negative images of ourselves with what God says about us.

You cannot unthink a thought! For example, if I ask you not to think about your favorite food, what are you going to think about? The more you say to yourself, "I am not going to think about my favorite food," guess what thoughts will start flooding your mind? We cannot unthink thoughts or unthink hurtful situations from our lives or past. So how do we change our thinking? By replacing those negative thoughts!

When you are struggling with hurtful, negative memories, replace those thoughts with the Word of God. If you start remembering a time when you gave into a temptation, flip the script on the devil. Begin to think and speak out loud a verse from the Bible, such as Psalm 103:12: "As far as the east is from the west, so far has he removed our transgressions from us." You would be amazed how powerful you could become if you took a walk every morning and quoted this verse out loud for at least fifteen minutes.

When you start thinking there is an area of your life that is doomed to failure, replace that discouraging thought with Philippians 4:13: "I can do all things through Christ who strengthens me." When you start replacing the negative with the powerful messages found in the Word of God, you will suddenly discover that your mind-set begins to change.

If you want your life to change, then you need to change your thinking. Ask God to help you line up your thinking with his Word. Don't let another day go by without uprooting and replacing every negative, hurtful thought from the devil with the life-giving truth found only in God's Word.

You May Be Living With A Problem, But Don't Let The Problem Live In You

The reality for the Israelites was they had to live with the fact that there was a person named Goliath, and he was their enemy. You may be living with a problem, but don't let the problem live in you. God's people could not put their heads in the sand and expect this nine-foot giant to leave. I wish we could simply ignore our problems, and they would just magically go away. But unfortunately, the opposite is true in that most of the time when we ignore our troubles, it can actually make those problems worse.

Once you realize there is a giant in your life, then you have to make a choice. Will you let this problem live in you? I implore you to say no. Don't let the problem live in you! You may be in a toxic environment at your work, school, or family, but choose not to allow that toxic environment to live in you.

Eleanor Roosevelt once said, "No one can make you feel inferior without your consent." Don't give your consent to the devil to ruin your life or hurt your family. Don't give your consent to the enemy to wreak havoc on your relationship with God and others. You may be living with a problem, but don't let the problem live in you.

You might be thinking, "Barry, that notion of not allowing a problem to live in me sounds good and all, but how do I make that a reality for my life?" The way you ensure that a problem doesn't live in you is by taking authority over it. As a child of God, you have his power and authority. You are a King's kid; therefore, you have access to the King of kings and the Lord of lords!

I have worked as a police chaplain for almost a decade. I have spent time with traffic officers who stand right in the middle of busy street intersections and raise their hands, which then causes three-thousand-pound cars to suddenly come to a stop. Why do the cars stop? Do police officers have Superman-like capabilities coming out of their hands to shut down the car engines? No! The people driving those cars stop for police officers because of the authority they carry. Consider what Ephesians 1:19–20 says: "That power is the same as the mighty strength he exerted when he raised Christ from the dead and seated him at his right hand in the heavenly realms." Wow, I love that verse!

Because you are a child of God, you have more power and authority than any police badge could ever produce. You are given the same power that raised Jesus from the dead. If Jesus overcame death, hell, and the grave, then you can overcome any pesky giant that the devil would try to put into your life. Always remember that you have authority!

All Christians have authority, but most don't know or understand that they do. One day, I was showing a friend of mine something I had recently bought that was stowed away in the back of my car. I opened up the trunk, laid my keys down to free up a hand, and then showed him this valuable article. As we were about to leave, I quickly shut the trunk and attempted to drive off, but to my horror, I realized I had locked the keys in the trunk. Ugh!

I was then forced to call someone to come and assist me with retrieving the keys that were locked in the car. I also asked my friend if he would be willing to wait with me until the locksmith showed up. Unfortunately, the locksmith couldn't open the right side of my car, so then he tried to open the left side of my car. Finally, after waiting for what seemed to be an eternity, he opened my car. Then, I had to pay him for assisting me with getting my keys out of the trunk. However, the story got worse. After the locksmith left, I suddenly remembered that I had roadside assistance with our insurance company. I just paid money to a locksmith for a service I already had for free. If I would have just called my insurance company, they would have sent someone out quicker, and I could have retrieved my keys for free!

This story is a picture of a Christian who doesn't take hold of the authority that is freely given to him or her through Jesus. He or she has access to God's power but instead turns to a different source. Or, just like how I was in this story, many Christians forget what they have. I wasted time and money on something I already possessed. Even though I forgot I had roadside assistance coverage, it doesn't change the fact that I still possessed it. As believers, we have access to so much, yet we often forget what God has given to us.

You can believe for the impossible! But in order to receive the impossible, you have to change your thinking. In order to have everything God wants you to have, you cannot allow the problems of life to live in you!

4

USE WEAPONS OF FAITH
EMPOWERED BY THE HOLY SPIRIT

*"So Saul clothed David with his armor, and he
put a bronze helmet on his head; he also clothed
him with a coat of mail."*

1 Samuel 17:38

*"And David said to Saul, 'I cannot walk with
these, for I have not tested them.' So David took
them off."*

1 Samuel 17:39

It has been said that the most important rule in a gunfight is to bring a gun! The weapons we use in a fight will almost always determine the outcome. You can have a strong warrior fight and be defeated by a weaker defender if that defender uses the right weapon in the battle.

I am convinced that more Christians would have victory in their lives if they would choose the right weapons. In a battle, the weapon selection is vital. If a country goes to war and engages in a battle on the sea, it needs to use destroyers and aircraft carriers. If a nation plans to fight in the air, it needs military jets and cargo planes. When a country is defending itself on the ground, tanks, jeeps, and other ground-fighting weapons are needed.

What weapons are you using to combat the devil? What weapons are you trusting in to give you victory in the battle for your future, marriage, or dreams? What kind of ammunition are you attacking the devil with when he comes against you? These are questions many Christians have not contemplated.

Many times as believers we are in a battle with the enemy and are constantly on the defensive. Instead of allowing the devil to attack you, would you consider living on the offensive and attack the devil? If you are going to attack the devil, you need to have the right weapons. Guns and knives will not work on this enemy. You need something more powerful. You need something that is not natural but supernatural. If you will pick up the weapon of faith and flow in the power of the Holy Spirit, you can defeat your giants.

God Isn't Limited By Anything Except Our Lack Of Faith

Can I challenge you to pick up the weapon of faith? Look at 1 Samuel 17:38–39: "So Saul clothed David with his armor, and he put a bronze helmet on his head; he also clothed him with a coat of mail." In verse 39, David states to Saul, "I cannot walk with these." David declined the king's weapons. Now consider that since King Saul was of royalty, it meant that he probably had amazing weapons of warfare that would have been considered the best of the best for that time period. Yet in spite of Saul having superior weapon quality, David opted for a much more powerful weapon: faith in God.

You might be asking, what is faith? According to Hebrews 11:1, "Now faith is the substance of things hoped for, the evidence of things not seen." Faith means having confidence in God and not trusting in our own skills and education. Faith is truly believing that God can do what he said he will do. Faith also means risk and trusting what we can't see.

The invisible is valuable. We can't see love, but we know it is the most powerful force on the planet. We can't see electricity, but we know it supplies power to the cities of millions. We can't see wind, yet we know tornadic winds can tear down structures and buildings, causing millions of dollars in damages.

I have heard many pastors make the following comment, and I agree: faith is a muscle. The more you use that muscle, the stronger it becomes. I had the incredible privilege to work for and serve under Pastor Bill Newby. Pastor Newby was and is a hero in the faith. He would often say a phrase that has been established deep within my spirit, and that was: "Feed your faith and doubt your doubts." There are many ways to strengthen our faith, but I believe faith building begins with this first step that we can learn from Pastor Newby. The concept is simple in that what we feed will grow. If you are feeding your faith with the Word of God, it will grow. If you are feeding your faith by spending quality time with passionate, on-fire-for-God believers, it will grow. Our faith must be fed and not starved.

When you choose not to go to church, you are starving your faith. When you don't spend daily time with God reading the Bible and praying, you are starving your faith. When you don't have believers in your life who can build you up and encourage you when times are tough, you are starving your faith.

The key to feeding your faith begins and ends with your daily quiet time with God. The vast majority of Christians don't read the Bible every day. If you are struggling with daily reading the Bible, I want to encourage you to get a book that God guided me to write called the *30 Second Devotional*. The idea for this devotional came from Psalm 34:8: "Oh, taste and see that the Lord is good; blessed is the man who trusts in him!" I challenge people to start spending 30 seconds with God every day, with the understanding that this 30-second time frame isn't the finish line but is the starting line. The goal is for people to taste and see that the Lord is good and to want more of him.

For many people, it might be difficult or even overwhelming to make time every day to spend an hour with God. But most people are able to start with 30 seconds per day and then let that time grow with God as they enjoy spending time in his presence. The key is that we all need to spend daily time with God in order to feed our faith. If you are interested in the *30 Second Devotional*, you can learn more at www.servingpastors.com.

All of us need to build our faith and meet alone with God every day. When we spend time in God's presence, he can heal the hurts of the day. When we get alone with

God, he can speak his truth and vision deep into our souls. When we are with our Heavenly Father, we get the privilege of spending time with the author and source of life.

As powerful as God is, our lack of faith will limit God from moving in our lives! For example, you can't be saved until you place your faith in Jesus. Oftentimes, we read in the New Testament where people were only made whole by their faith. For instance, in Mark 5:34, Jesus tells a woman who had a bleeding illness for many years, "Daughter, your faith has healed you. Go in peace and be freed from your suffering." God was able to move in her life and bring healing because she had faith. Therefore, the Creator of the universe can be limited by our lack of faith, so it is important to make sure we are daily feeding our faith and doubting our doubts!

God Wants You To Focus On What He Can Do, Not On What You Can't Do

It would have been really easy for David to trust in what he saw: the magnificent weapons of King Saul. But instead, David was more focused on what God could do and not on what he couldn't do. David trusted God to do what only he could do!

The trap of the devil is to get you focused on your own limitations and shortcomings. The devil wants you to think you are not educated enough, you don't have the right connections, or you don't have enough skill or ability to do what God has called you to do. He might be right, since human beings do have limitations, but as a Christian, the most important thing you do have is your relationship with God! That relationship is the only thing you need because you have access to your supernatural, loving Heavenly Father.

God wants you focused on what he can do, not on what you can't do. Consider and reflect on what God can do:

- Forgive our sins (1 John 1:9)
- Heal our sickness and diseases (Isaiah 53:5)
- Raise the dead (Mark 5:42)
- Part the seas (Exodus 14:21)
- Give us peace during the storms of life (Matthew 8:26)
- Bring comfort and give us joy (Psalm 147:3)
- Help a man walk on water (Matthew 14:29)
- Provide for our needs supernaturally (John 6:13)
- Bring hope and possibility (Luke 18:27)
- Make all things new (Revelation 21:5)
- Save our souls (John 3:16)

The Bible is full of stories about God miraculously providing for his people. In fact, in John 21:25, it states, "And there are also many other things that Jesus did, which if they were written one by one, I suppose that even the world itself could not contain the books that would be written." God is so good!

If you are focused on what you can't do, you will never have victory in life. If you are focused on what you can't accomplish, you will never see the dreams and visions God has for you become a reality. The trick of the devil is to get you focused on you.

However, if you will focus on what only God can do, you can slay the giants in your life! David had the victory way before he ever stepped into the ring to face Goliath. David already became the champion and defeated the nine-foot-tall giant way before he ever picked up his slingshot. Why? Because David was more focused on what God could do than on what he could not do. He knew with God he would always have the victory, and the same can be said today that when we trust God, we will have certain victory too!

You are filled with possibilities! But in order to make those possibilities a reality, you can't be consumed with your own limitations; instead, you must be consumed with what God can do!

5

BRING YOUR CONFIRMATION NUMBERS

"For the battle is the Lord's."

1 Samuel 17:47

David faced Goliath, but he was confident that the battle was in God's hands. When we face the day-to-day trials, issues, and hang-ups in life, we need to know that even in our small or large issues we can be confident in God.

When my wife and I lived in Southern California, we had the privilege of taking a trip along the California coast for an extended weekend getaway. What made this trip even more enjoyable was that we had collected enough reward points to earn a free hotel stay at a historic beachfront property. When I had redeemed our points to make the reservation online, I received an e-mail with a confirmation number for my free night's stay. I almost shut down my computer, but something prompted me to print off a hard copy of the room information and the confirmation number.

After a long season of hard work, my wife and I set off for our extended weekend getaway. We drove up Big Sur on our way to San Francisco. We had a great time in Frisco and then were heading back to Southern California. On our last night's stay, we were finally ready to cash in on our free hotel room in this beautiful beach community. It was a nice hotel, well-kept, and right off the Pacific Ocean. Vacationing in California is absolutely beautiful, but it can be expensive, so we were excited about our free stay!

When we arrived, we went to the front desk to check in to our free room. As we were checking in, the front-desk

clerk told us the hotel was recently under new manage-
ment, and that they required advance payment for the
room. I notified her that we had a free room and gave
her my first and last name. After some checking, she said
she had my name, but she mentioned she would still need
to charge me because she had no record of me redeem-
ing points for a free room. I explained to her that I was
a rewards member and even tried to give her my rewards
number. Still, I could not convince her to give me the free
room that was legally mine.

After some frustrating dialogue with the front-desk
clerk, I suddenly remembered that I had printed off the
confirmation number. I told her I had one last thing I
needed to show her to hopefully convince her to give me
the room at no charge. I opened up my bag and pulled out
the copy of the e-mail, which had the name of the hotel,
my name, and most importantly, the confirmation number
for my free night's stay. It was like a tidal wave had hit,
because her face and tone changed right before my eyes.
Before I knew it, I had my key and was on my way to un-
pack in my free room!

When I was debating with this hotel desk clerk, I
couldn't win the case. Even when I showed her my rewards number along with a photo ID, I couldn't persuade
her. But, when I pulled out the confirmation number, no

matter how badly she didn't want to give me a free room, she knew she had to because it was a promise in writing. She was obligated under the legal power of the document and the confirmation number to give me my free night's stay. What is the point of me telling you this story? This account is a picture of our own struggle with the devil. When we debate him, we will lose every time. When we talk to the devil about who we are in our own power, we can't do anything. However, everything changes when we have a confirmation number from the Word of God that confirms authority. You and I have confirmation numbers. When the devil attacks, you give him one or more of these confirmation numbers from the Bible:

- When you are tempted: "No temptation has over-taken you" (1 Corinthians 10:13).
- When you feel guilty: "[God] forgives all your in-iquities" (Psalm 103:3).
- When you don't believe you can be victorious: "I can do all things through Christ who strengthens me" (Philippians 4:13).
- When you fail: "There is therefore now no condem-nation to those who are in Christ Jesus" (Romans 8:1).
- When you need healing: "And by His stripes we are healed" (Isaiah 53:5).

- When you need encouragement for success: "Commit your works to the Lord, and your thoughts will be established" (Proverbs 16:3).
- When you need reassurance that you are saved: "For whoever calls on the name of the Lord shall be saved" (Romans 10:13).
- When you are facing difficult trials: "Yea, though I walk through the valley of the shadow of death, I will fear no evil" (Psalm 23:4).
- When you doubt God's love: "Behold what manner of love the Father has bestowed on us" (1 John 3:1).
- When you need strength: "'Not by might nor by power, but by My Spirit,' says the Lord of hosts" (Zechariah 4:6).
- When everything is against you: "No weapon formed against you shall prosper" (Isaiah 54:17).
- When you don't think you can be forgiven: "If we confess our sins, He is faithful and just to forgive us our sins and to cleanse us from all unrighteousness" (1 John 1:9).
- When you are tempted to give up on your marriage: "Love never fails" (1 Corinthians 13:8).

The Bible is packed with God's truth and promises that we all need to memorize and quote to the devil when he attacks us. The above verses are just a small list to help you get started as you study God's Word and write down promises/confirmation numbers for your life.

You might be thinking this business of confirmation numbers is crazy. Well, Jesus didn't think so! In Matthew 4:1–11, Jesus is attacked and tempted by the devil for forty days in the wilderness. Jesus lived a perfect life and never sinned. How did he overcome the three temptations the devil tried to hurl at him? In Matthew 4:4, 4:7, and 4:10, Jesus said, "It is written" and let the devil have it with the Word of God. Jesus quoted the Word to the devil. Jesus gave the devil three different confirmation numbers to combat the three temptations! If it worked for Jesus, it will work for you too.

As you finish reading this book, be aware that if the devil is attacking your life, you are probably doing something right. As long as we live on this earth, we will always have to combat and resist the devil. But we can have the victory! At times, we are going to fall short, but we can still rise up and walk in victory. We will not attain perfection on this side of heaven; however, Jesus does promise to give us the abundant life.

Would you make a decision today? Would you agree with Jesus in John 10:10, when he says, "I have come that they may have life, and that they may have it more abundantly"? Would you walk away from the absent life and run to the abundant life that is found only in Jesus? You can have victory in your life. I plead with you not to give up. Don't give up on your life, vision, marriage, goals, and lastly, on your God-given dreams. Walk in the victory God has already given to you. Live life on the offensive!

WHAT TO LEAVE WITH

God wants you to have victory in your life. However, what God desires for our life does not always happen. The Bible states in 2 Peter 3:9, "The Lord is not slack concerning his promise, as some count slackness, but is longsuffering toward us, not willing that any should perish but that all should come to repentance." However, do people die without having a personal relationship with Jesus? Sadly, the answer is yes. Do Christians live their lives with less power than what God would like them to have? Again, disappointingly, yes. There is much that happens in this fallen world that is not in God's will and that deeply hurts his heart.

If you want to have victory in your life, you have to step out in faith and take hold of it. You have to boldly declare the Word of God over your life. You have to refuse to quit. Consider these three faith steps that are essential to walking in victory:

- **See it.** You have to see what others can't see.
- **Say it.** You have to boldly declare God's Word over your situations.
- **Seize it.** You have to victoriously take hold of what God has promised you.

Let me leave you with this final thought: the person who determines if you will have victory in your life isn't your pastor, family or friends, it is *you*! Victory in life is a choice. Choose to have God's victory today!

Books by Barry Young

30 Second Devotional

30 Second Devotional for First Responders

How to Have Victory in Life

How to Live a Life of Blessing

To learn more about Barry Young or Serving Pastors Ministries, visit www.servingpastors.com.

62197302R00035

Made in the USA
Middletown, DE
19 January 2018